Depth Studies

Britain
and the
Slave Trade

Rosemary Rees

Heinemann

Heinemann Library,
Halley Court, Jordan Hill, Oxford OX2 8EJ
a division of Reed Educational and Professional
Publishing Ltd

OXFORD LONDON EDINBURGH MADRID
ATHENS BOLOGNA PARIS MELBOURNE
SYDNEY AUCKLAND SINGAPORE TOKYO
IBADAN NAIROBI HARARE GABORONE
PORTSMOUTH NH (USA)

First published 1995
This edition 1996

00 99 98 97 96 10 9 8 7 6 5 4 3 2 1

**British Library Cataloguing Data is available
from the British Library on request.**

ISBN 0 431 07076 8
This book is also available in a hardback library
edition (ISBN 0 431 07069 5)

Designed by Ron Kamen, Green Door Design Ltd,
Basingstoke
Illustrated by Jeff Edwards
Printed in Spain by Mateu Cromo

Front cover: A painting by a British naval officer,
showing slaves below deck.

Acknowledgements

The author and publisher would like to thank the
following for permission to reproduce photographs:
The Bridgeman Art Library: 1.8
The Bridgeman Art Library/British Library: 2.5, 2.8
The Bridgeman Art Library/British Museum: 1.1
The Bridgeman Art Library/City of Bristol Museum
and Art Gallery: 3.4
Cambridge University Press / Royal Geographical
Collection: 3.1
Mary Evans Picture Library: 4.8
E.T. Archive: 2.3
Fotomas Index: 2.11
Guildhall Library, Corporation of London: 3.7
The Billie Love Historical Collection: 4.11
The Mansell Collection: 1.4, 4.5
The Menil Collection, Houston / Hickey-Robertson: 2.14
National Library of Jamaica: 2.16
National Maritime Museum, London: Front cover
National Portrait Gallery: 4.7
Peter Newark's American Pictures: 2.1
The Trustees of the Wedgwood Museum, Barlaston,
Staffordshire: 4.4

Every effort has been made to contact copyright
holders of material published in this book. Any
omissions will be rectified in subsequent printings if
notice is given to the publisher.

Details of written sources

In some sources the wording or sentence structure has
been simplified to ensure that the source is accessible.

J. W. Arrowsmith, *Bristol Past and Present*, Bristol,
1881–2: 3.3
William Bosman, *A New and Accurate Description of
the Coast of Guinea*, London, 1705: 1.6
Mrs. Carmichael, *Domestic Manners - Social
Conditions of the Population of the West Indies*, Negro
Universities Press, 1969: 2.9, 2.13
L. Comitas and D. Lowenthal, *Slaves, Free Men,
Citizens*, Anchor Books, 1973: 2.15
W. H. B. Court, *The Rise of the Midland Industries*,
1938: 3.5
M. Cranton, J. Walvin and D. Wright, *Slavery,
Abolition and Emancipation*, Longman, 1976: 4.3
William Dickinson, *Mitigation of Slavery*, 1814: 2.6
Bryan Edwards, *History of the British Colonies in the
West Indies*, London, 1801: 2.12
Olaudah Equiano, *The Interesting Narrative of the Life
of Olaudah Equiano*, London, 1789: 1.5, 1.7, 1.7, 2.2
Peter Fryer, *Staying Power: The History of Black
People in Britain*, Pluto, 1984: 4.1, 4.2
C. L. R. James, *The Black Jacobins*, Allison and Busby,
1980: 2.7, 4.9
John Matthews, *A Voyage on the river Sierra Leone on
the Coast of Africa*, London, 1788: 1.3
Ramsey Muir, *A History of Liverpool*, 1907: 3.2
Lady Nugent, *Lady Nugent's Journal of her Residence in
Jamaica from 1801–5*, Institute of Jamaica, 1966: 2.10
Malachy Postlethwayt, *The African Trade, the Great
Pillar and Support of the British Plantation Trade in
America*, J. Robinson, 1746: 3.6
Sackville-West, *Knoll and the Sackvilles*, 1922: 4.6
James Walvin, *Black Ivory*, HarperCollins, 1992: 1.2, 2.4

Note

In this book some of the words are printed in **bold**
type. This indicates that the word is listed in the
glossary on pages 30–1. The glossary gives a brief
explanation of words that may be new to you.

Contents

What was the Slave Trade?

Many peoples in the past used **slaves** to work for them. Slaves helped to build the pyramids of ancient Egypt; slaves worked for the ancient Greeks in their fields and in their homes; slaves rowed galleys for the Romans and helped build aqueducts and roads. At the time of the Industrial Revolution the British, and other Europeans, traded in slaves. Merchants bought and sold people just as they bought and sold other goods like cotton, fish, wood, guns and saucepans.

Why did British merchants buy and sell African people?

By 1750 there were nearly 600 coffee houses in London. They were places where men read the daily papers, plotted against their political rivals, carried out business deals and passed on gossip and hard information about goings-on in far corners of the British Empire. Coffee was a new drink, and coffee houses could not exist, of course, if coffee had not been grown in the **West Indies** and shipped to Britain. Coffee was not the only new drink in Britain. Tea from China (and later from India) and chocolate from Africa and America were very popular. Coffee, tea and chocolate, however, tasted bitter. They all needed sugar to make them taste good. British people needed sugar for more than sweetening drinks. They made all kinds of sweet puddings: pies and tarts, creams and trifles. By 1800 the British were using a great deal more sugar than they had in 1650. This sugar came from the **British West Indies**. The sugar cane **plantations** were worked by black slaves, taken there from Africa by British merchants.

A picture of a London coffee house, painted in 1705.

Growth in Trade

Sugar poured into Britain for immediate use and for re-export to other European countries. In 1775, for example, the British West Indies produced 100,000 tons of sugar. British merchants made huge profits, which they either spent on houses and land, or invested in industry and business. Industry boomed; more and more ships were built and trade flourished; small ports and towns grew into international trading centres. Underpinning all this prosperity was the slave trade.

The slave trade was part of a much larger enterprise called the Triangular Trade, which was made up of three separate voyages. The three voyages of the triangle are shown on the map. It usually took about eleven months to complete the three journeys. Look carefully at the map and you will see that under this system no ship ever sailed empty. In this way the ships' owners made vast profits.

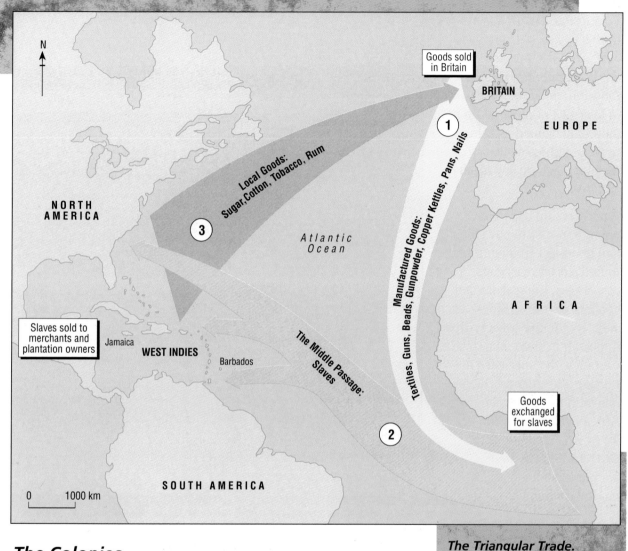

The Triangular Trade.

The Colonies

British **colonies** were not independent countries. They belonged to Britain. The money to run them and defend them came from British taxes. So the British government believed it had the right to control trade to and from British colonies. Parliament passed a series of **Navigation Laws**. These laws said that all trade to and from the colonies had to be carried in British ships; that the colonies could buy manufactured goods only from Britain and that the colonies could not sell goods like sugar, tobacco and cotton to any country outside the British Empire.

PITT

William Pitt (1759–1806) was the younger son of the Earl of Chatham. He was a lawyer and was elected as an MP in 1781. In 1782 he was made Chancellor of the Exchequer. Two year later he was made Prime Minister – the youngest ever. He was Prime Minister from 1784–1801 and from 1804–6. He agreed with William Wilberforce's campaign against the slave trade and helped all he could.

5

Sailing to Africa

British merchants prepared very carefully for their sailings to Africa. **The Triangular Trade** was a tricky business. There were vast profits to be made, but if the preparations were not thorough enough, it was easy to lose a lot of money. Often, merchants joined together in partnerships so that they could share any profits and losses.

A partnership had to have enough money to buy ships and goods for trading. It had to find a crew: surgeons, carpenters, sail-makers and coopers (barrel makers), as well as ordinary sailors. Most importantly, there had to be a captain with experience in dealing with African chiefs and with merchants on the African coast, and who knew what conditions to expect when the ship anchored at one of the coastal trading forts.

It was very important that ships arrived on the African coast at the right time. Ships' captains had to leave enough time to pick up a full load of slaves, while at the same time making sure they arrived in the Caribbean with time to sell them and pick up a cargo of sugar or tobacco or cotton while it was in good condition. It was a mistake, for example, to arrive off the coast of Africa in the rainy season. Not only would many crew members fall ill, but African traders could not move slaves easily to the coast. Most ships left British ports between July and September and aimed to get to the Caribbean by the end of the following April, which was sugar-making time.

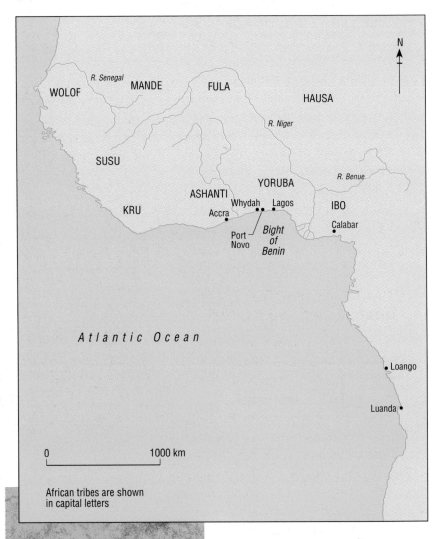

This map shows the part of Africa where the British and other Europeans traded for slaves.

SOURCE 2

Beware and take care
Of the Bight [bay] of Benin.
For one that comes out
There are forty go in.

An old rhyme warning about the fate of many sailors when their ships anchored off the coast of Africa. About 2 million slaves, one-fifth of all those shipped across the Atlantic, came from this area.

There were two main ways of trading for slaves once ships reached the African coast. Some British merchants had **agents** working for them in Africa. These agents usually lived in European trading posts on the coast. They had a complicated network of African contacts and dealers stretching far inland. This meant that an agent could have a cargo of African slaves ready and waiting for the slave ship to arrive. Not all merchants had agents. Some **slavers** simply sailed along the coast, buying slaves where they could, until they had a full cargo and could set sail across the Atlantic.

Where did the African traders and dealers get the slaves?

Africans who became slaves were often captured in war by other African tribes. Some were kidnapped. Some were thrown out of their tribes because they had committed a crime; others were thrown out of their tribes because they had offended against tribal customs. A girl who began her monthly periods too early, a woman who gave birth to twins or a man who had sex with a woman who was not his wife were all sold by their tribes into slavery.

SOURCE 4

A painting of African slaves being driven to the coast.

SOURCE 5

When the grown people were gone far in the fields to labour, the children assembled together to play; and usually some of us used to get up a tree to look out for any assailant or kidnapper that might come upon us; for they sometimes took these opportunities of our parents' absence, to attack and carry off as many as they could seize.

*This was written by Olaudah Equiano. When he was a child he was kidnapped from his village in Africa and sold into slavery. In 1789, when he was a free man, he wrote a book about his life. It is called **The Interesting Narrative of the Life of Olaudah Equiano**. It is an important book because it is almost the only account we have from someone who was actually a slave.*

SOURCE 3

The best information I have been able to collect is that great numbers are prisoners taken in war and brought down, fifty or a hundred together, by the black slave merchant.

*Written by John Matthews, an Englishman who traded for slaves in Sierra Leone in his book, **A Voyage on the river Sierra Leone on the Coast of Africa**, published in London in 1788.*

How did British merchants buy African people?

All slavers needed a licence from a local chief before they could trade. Getting a licence was a complicated business, and involved either paying certain fees to the local chief, or agreeing with the chief to buy a certain number of slaves at a set price. Slave traders could never be sure exactly what a chief would ask for. They had to be ready to meet almost any request so that they did not risk the whole of the rest of their Triangular Trade. By the end of the 1700s each slave ship had to pay out about £400 in presents and fees before the captain was allowed to buy slaves.

Europeans were not allowed to travel inland to buy slaves. African traders always brought the slaves to trading posts on the coast. There, British merchants and captains inspected men, women and children very carefully. Merchants would not buy a slave if they found anything wrong. The voyage across the Atlantic was going to be bad enough: only slaves who were fit and healthy at the start stood a chance of surviving. Gradually a full cargo of slaves (usually about 450 people) was put together, and the dreadful Atlantic crossing began. Slaves who were rejected by the merchants were either killed or used as slaves by black Africans.

How did British merchants sell slaves in the Caribbean?

Most slaves suffered terribly on the journey across the Atlantic, and many died. The merchants and **planters** waiting in the West Indies for the slavers to arrive were very well aware that disease and illness thrived in ships' holds. They would buy only strong, healthy-looking slaves. It was up to the ships' captains to make sure the slaves they were selling looked as fit as possible. All slaves were given water to wash in, and palm oil to rub on their skins. This gave them a shiny, healthy look. Grey hair was dyed black to make the slaves look younger. Slaves often had **dysentery**. One ship's captain ordered his slaves' anuses to be plugged with rope so that the customers would not know what was wrong with them.

Slave traders wanted the best prices for their slaves. They preferred to sell their cargo at one port only, but if prices were low or if some slaves were left unsold, slave captains sailed from island to island, selling a few slaves at each port.

SOURCE 6

When slaves are brought from the inland countries, they are put in prison together. When we buy them, they are all brought out together and thoroughly examined by our surgeons. Those which are approved as good are set on one side; in the meantime a burning iron, with the name of the company, lies in the fire. With this iron ours are marked on the chest after we have agreed a price with the owners of the slaves.

> *From the book **A New and Accurate Description of the Coast of Guinea,** published in 1705. It was written by William Bosman, a slave trader.*

SOURCE 7

On a signal given [the beat of a drum] the buyers rushed into the yard where the slaves were confined, and chose the ones they liked best. The noise and clamour, and the eagerness shown on the faces of the buyers, increased the fear of the terrified Africans. In this way, relations and friends were separated, most of them never to see each other again.

> *Olaudah Equiano describes a 'scramble'. He was sold at a 'scramble' when his slave ship landed in Barbados.*

This slave family is being auctioned in Virginia, USA, in the nineteenth century.

The captains of slave ships had three main ways of selling their cargo. They could sell the slaves by **private treaty**; they could sell the slaves in a 'scramble', or they could sell the slaves in a public **auction.** They usually sold slaves to merchants who sold them on to planters. Sometimes they sold direct to planters. Slaves sold by private treaty were usually the healthiest and they went first. They were sold directly to planters, or to '**middlemen**' who sold them on, at a price that had been agreed earlier. A 'scramble' was, perhaps, the most frightening way of being sold (read Source 7). What actually happened was that the slavers agreed a price per slave with the merchants who were buying. It was then up to the merchants to grab as many slaves as they could. There were always slaves left over: those who were not bought for some reason or other. These were called the '**refuse slaves**'. Because no one wanted to buy them, they were usually sold at a public auction.

SANCHO

Ignatius Sancho (1729–80) was born on a slave ship. His mother died when he was born. His father killed himself rather than live as a slave. When Sancho was two his owner took him to England and sold him to three sisters who lived in Greenwich, London. They did not believe in educating slaves. A neighbour, the Duke of Montagu, took an interest in Sancho and lent him books. He later went to work for the Montagus. Sancho married and had six children. When he was freed he ran a grocery shop in Westminster, London. He wrote poetry and plays and had many famous friends.

What was life like for black slaves?

The Middle Passage

The crossing from Africa to the Americas was called the **Middle Passage**. It took slave ships between forty and sixty-nine days to make the voyage. Most slaves suffered terribly, and many died.

On the day a slave ship was due to sail, the sailors loaded their cargo of slaves. As soon as the slaves got on board they were stripped naked; men and women were put into separate **holds**, and the men were chained together in pairs by their ankles.

The holds were about 1.52 metres high, and on some ships carpenters built half decks along the sides so as to pack in more slaves. Once the slave ship sailed, the women and children were usually allowed to stay on deck. Here the air was fresher than in the holds, but there were only tarpaulins to protect them from the wind, rain and sun.

Every day there was the same routine. Sailors washed the slaves down first thing in the morning, and then inspected them to see whether or not they had any illnesses. Slaves were cargo, and had to arrive in good condition if the merchants were to make high profits and the sailors' wages were to be paid. The slaves ate in the morning and afternoon, and had half a pint of water twice a day. Their meals consisted mainly of rice, **yams** and **horse-beans** all mashed together, and sometimes covered with 'slabber-sauce', which was a mixture of palm oil, water and pepper. Slaves ate in groups, and often the groups were led by a kind of monitor, who told the slaves when to pick up the food, when to put it in their mouths and when to swallow.

SOURCE 1

Sailors putting slaves into the hold of a slave ship.

SOURCE 2

The stench of the hold, the heat and the crowding, which meant that each had scarcely room to turn, almost suffocated us. There was sickness among the slaves of which many died. The situation was aggravated by the rubbing of the chains and the filth of the lavatory-buckets into which children often fell. I became so sick that, as I was a young boy, my chains were removed and I was allowed to stay on deck. One day, two of my wearied countrymen who were chained together, preferring death to such a life of misery, jumped into the sea.

From **The Interesting Narrative of the Life of Olaudah Equiano** by himself, published in 1789. Look back at page 7, where you will read more about Olaudah Equiano.

Many slaves found the food revolting and refused to eat. When this happened, sailors used mouth openers to force food down their throats. At sunset, the **boatswain** and **second mate** went down into the holds with whips to settle the slaves down for the night. The tallest slept in the middle of the ship, and the shortest in the **bow.** Slaves on the right-hand side of a ship faced forward and lay in each other's laps; slaves on the left-hand side of a ship faced the **stern.** The sailors put large buckets in the hold for the slaves to use as lavatories, but because the slaves were chained together and packed in tightly, many of them couldn't get to the nearest bucket in time.

It was not surprising that many slaves fell ill. There was very little fresh air in the holds: most slave ships had only six **portholes** along each side of the hull. Many slaves got seasick and developed **heat stroke**. They were packed together in cramped and filthy holds, and disease spread quickly. At this time, no one knew exactly how disease spread, and so no one knew what to do to stop it spreading. Slaves developed fevers, where they had high temperatures and shivered and sweated. They developed dysentery, which meant they had diarrhoea which did not stop. Worse than this, they sometimes caught smallpox. A cargo of slaves with **smallpox** was a disaster for the slaves themselves and for the merchants. There was no cure, and many died. Dead slaves were thrown overboard, and provided food for the sharks.

Many slaves tried to end their own lives. Some hanged themselves; others jumped overboard. Some slaves reacted differently. They fought with their ship's captain and crew. Their aim was to take over the ship. This was not always a difficult thing to do. Most ships had only ten sailors to every hundred slaves, and some **mutinies** were successful (see Source 3).

SOURCE **3**

A picture of what most sailors feared: a slave mutiny. Historians have calculated that there was a slave revolt on a British slaver once every two years.

SOURCE **4**

Made a timely discovery today that the slaves were forming a plot for insurrection. Surprised two of them in getting off their irons. Put the boys in irons and slightly in thumbscrews to urge them to a full confession.

Thursday 23 May	Buried a man slave (No 34)
Wednesday 29 May	Buried a boy slave (No 86) of a flux [fever]
Wednesday 12 June	Buried a man slave (No 84) of a flux, which he had been struggling with near 7 weeks
Thursday 13 June	This morning buryed a woman slave (No47) Know not what she died of for she has not been properly alive since she first came on board.

These are extracts from the log of a slave captain, John Newton. He wrote it during a voyage from Sierra Leone to Antigua in 1751.

What was a sugar plantation like?

By the end of the 1700s the average sugar plantation spread over about 900 **acres**. Roughly 300 acres were for growing sugar cane; 300 acres of woodland and 300 acres for growing food. As well as the fields, plantations also had the estate house for the owner and his family, huts for the slaves to live in, and a range of buildings (for example, a mill, boiling-house, still, drying-house, sheds, storehouses) for processing the sugar cane into sugar and for making sugar's by-product, rum.

Why were slaves necessary?

When the British first settled in the Caribbean in the 1600s and began to grow tobacco, cotton and sugar, black African slaves worked in the fields with white European labourers. Gradually, fewer white people wanted to work as labourers in the Caribbean. At the same time, the settlers started to grow more sugar. British demand for sugar grew, and the settlers got good prices for their sugar. Sugar plantations needed a lot of labourers, and so the owners bought more Africans from the slave traders. The owners needed cheap labour so that they could make large profits. Slaves, once they had been bought, worked for nothing. They belonged to the plantation owners just like any other possession. Because they were regarded as possessions, slaves had no rights at all. Owners could treat their slaves exactly as they pleased. They could, and many did, work or whip them to death. By the beginning of the 1700s, there were far more black Africans in the Caribbean than there were white people. The plantation owners grew afraid that their black African slaves would turn against them. They treated their slaves harshly, and controlled them through fear.

SOURCE 5

A picture of slaves cutting the sugar cane on a plantation in Jamaica painted in 1823 by W. Clark.

SOURCE 6

The general power which a Master exercises, and permits to be exercised over his slaves, is rather by implication [from slaves being bought as **chattels**, in the same manner as horses or other beasts] than by any positive law defining what the power of a master shall be.

William Dickinson wrote this in 1814. He was secretary to the Governor of Barbados in the 1700s.

THINK IT THROUGH

The plantation owners wanted to get the very best work from their slaves. Why, then, did some owners beat their slaves to death?

What work did the slaves do on the plantations?

Field labourers worked from dawn until sunset. They dug, hoed, weeded, planted and manured the sugar canes. Men and women worked together in gangs. **Overseers** organized **gangs** of child slaves to do the weeding. All the slave gangs had to work at the same speed, and the overseers used their whips to make quite sure they did. The busiest time in the fields was during 'crop' when the sugar cane was harvested and it was quite usual for slaves to work 18–20 hours a day. Slaves loaded the cut cane on to carts. They took the cane to the mill where it was crushed to get the juice out. Slaves boiled the juice until it turned into a thick brown liquid which they poured into barrels called hogsheads. The hogsheads were stored until brown sticky syrup called **molasses** could be drawn off, and only sugar was left behind. The barrels were then sealed, and shipped back to England. Slaves mixed water and yeast with the molasses and left the mixture to ferment and change into rum. Plantation owners made huge profits from both the sugar and the rum.

Domestic slaves had to work whatever hours their owners wanted them to. In some ways their position was better than the field slaves. They often had better food and were sometimes given cast-off clothes to wear. However, women and girls had to say 'Yes' to whatever sexual advances the owner and other white men wanted to make. If they refused, they would be punished and at the very least be sent back to work in the fields.

SOURCE 7

They were about a hundred men and women of different ages, all occupied in digging ditches in a cane-field, the majority of them naked or covered with rags. The sun shone down with full force on their heads. Sweat rolled from all parts of their bodies. Their limbs, weighed down by the heat, fatigued with the weight of their picks and by the resistance of the clayey soil baked hard enough to break their implements, strained themselves to overcome every obstacle. A mournful silence reigned. Exhaustion was stamped on every face, but the hour of rest had not yet come. Several foremen armed with long whips moved periodically between them, giving stinging blows to all who, worn out by fatigue, were compelled to take a rest.

A Swiss traveller, Girod-Chantrans, describes his visit to the Caribbean in 1785.

SOURCE 8

A picture of slaves working in a sugar boiling-house painted in 1823 by W. Clark.

THINK IT THROUGH

What are the differences between what Source 5 shows and what Source 7 says? Why do you think there are these differences?

What was life like amongst the slaves?

There were different levels within slave societies. At the very top came the highly skilled slaves, especially those who were allowed by their masters to earn some money of their own. Next came the slaves who were 'drivers' on plantations – those who used whips to drive other slaves to do their work. Of the same status with these slaves were the African priests who taught African religions which were usually forbidden by white masters. House slaves came next: they often had white fathers and black mothers and were called **mulattos.** Then came slaves with special skills: herbalists, nurses, potters and cabinet-makers. Finally, at the bottom of the heap, came the field workers. As well as all this, slaves who had been born in the West Indies (called **creoles**) were usually regarded as better than those who had been born in Africa and shipped across the Atlantic. The slave owners did all they could to encourage these divisions between slaves.

Slaves spoke many different languages because they came from many different African tribes. Once in the West Indies, they had to develop a new language so that they could talk to each other and to their masters. They used African grammar and African and English words. Today some West Indians still speak **English creole**.

All the old African family ways were destroyed by slavery. Families were often split up when they were sold. Even families who managed to stay together, or men and women who set up new families in the Caribbean, could not be sure that they would stay together and bring up children together. Fathers and mothers were sold separately, sometimes to estates hundreds of miles apart, whenever a plantation owner thought it was a good commercial move to do so. Babies were often taken away from their mothers soon after birth and sold. Some mothers deliberately aborted their pregnancies and others killed their new-born babies to stop this happening. Gradually slaves developed a system whereby an older slave, called a **god-parent**, was responsible for the well-being of a younger slave, whether or not they were related.

SOURCE 9

The houses are built some of stone, some of wood, while others are wove like basket work. They thatch them neatly. The area varies from fifteen feet by twenty to twenty feet by thirty. The floor is generally earthen. Negroes of rank have bedsteads with mosquito curtains, their bedding being for the most part a bag filled with the dried plantain leaf. They have a blanket and pillows of the same materials; blankets, a good sheet, a good table, one or two benches and some chairs, a box of clothes. They cook in a little thatched shed not attached to their houses. The cooking utensils are very few and simple, consisting of two or three iron pots and a strong wooden pestle and mortar for beating the boiled plantain to a mash. A common field negro has only a bed, table and bench with cooking utensils.

Written by Mrs Carmichael in a book published in 1833. She was writing about Jamaica in the 1820s, when she was living there.

SOURCE 10

Captain Dobbin [a white man] died without seeing his children, and it is said has left all he is worth to his black mistress and her child. This is, I am afraid, too common a case in Jamaica.

Lady Nugent wrote this in her journal. She was the wife of the Governor of Jamaica 1801–5.

Slaves loved making music. They danced and sang at ceremonies and festivals; they sang working songs in the fields, and special songs to greet new masters. Their instruments were mostly homemade: drums, banjos, mandolins, rattles, pipes and whistles made from wood and string, gourds and hollow sugar cane. Often slaves used their music to mock and ridicule the whites.

Millions of slaves suffered terrible illnesses and died young. In 1792 half of the slaves bought by Worthy Park, a plantation in Jamaica, were dead four years later. One of the main problems was that the slave ships brought with them all the African killer diseases and these then mixed with the illnesses of Europe and America with dreadful results.

SOURCE 11

A picture of Slaves dancing and making music.

Estates doctors were usually helped by a local nurse, often a slave, who lived on the plantation. Most doctors tried their best, but often they did not know what to do to cure the sick slaves. They used the best European medicine, but this was often useless against tropical diseases. The slaves themselves sometimes used old tribal remedies, and these often worked better than western medicines. Slaves died from African diseases like **yaws**; from European diseases like measles and whooping cough; and from **dropsy** and dysentery. When slaves died, their deaths were written in the plantation slave book. The owner had lost a piece of property which would have to be replaced.

SOURCE 12

Their music consisted of Gambys [drums], shaky-shekies and kitty-katties; the latter is nothing but a flat piece of board with two sticks, the former is a bladder with a parcel of pebbles in it. But the main part of the music to which they dance is vocal; one girl generally singing two lines by herself, and being answered by the chorus.

*Bryan Edwards wrote this in his book **History of the British Colonies in the West Indies**, which was published in 1801.*

BARBER

Francis Barber (1735–1801) was born a slave in Jamaica. His owner brought him to England and sent him to school. When his owner died, in 1752, his Will set Barber free. He worked as a servant for Dr Samuel Johnson until Johnson died in 1782. Then he and his wife ran a school near Lichfield.

Resistance, runaways and punishment

Most Africans hated the way they were treated. Many of them protested against their treatment in whatever ways they could. They weren't paid for the work they did, so some worked as slowly as they dared; there were many unexplained 'accidents': wheels came off carts, tools broke, china plates fell off shelves and instructions were misunderstood. Some slaves went further and tried to poison their owners, set fire to their sugar canes and burn down their houses. Often the owners did not realize what was really happening. They just thought their slaves were stupid or lazy, or both. Owners who did realize what was happening, punished their slaves harshly.

Most of the British colonies had their own **assemblies**. Only rich whites could stand for election and vote in elections. The Caribbean Island Assemblies passed laws that meant the masters had total power over their slaves. The British government approved all these laws.

There was a dinner given by a club, to the ladies of Kingstown [St Vincent]. Mrs W took the trouble of seeing the arrangements made for supper; and one negro boy was left in the upper gallery, where it was laid out, to take care of it. After the dancing had ended, the party went on up to supper, but alas! supper there was none; every article had disappeared; there was nothing left but a few empty platters. This was rather a daring piece of impudence; but the lesser kinds of impudence are common wherever there are negro servants.

Written by Mrs Carmichael, a British woman who lived in the West Indies 1820–32.

This picture of a 'driver' whipping a slave was painted in 1849 by Marcel-Antoine Verdier.

Many slaves tried to run away, and some were successful. They fled from the British Caribbean islands by stowing away in boats which were sailing to Spanish colonies. Spanish colonies used slaves but they never returned runaways. Some slaves made it to America where they were smuggled along the '**underground railroad**' to the northern states where they would be free. Some runaway slaves became pirates. In Jamaica many fled to the mountains and joined earlier runaways: the **Maroons,** who had fled from the invading British in 1655. Captured runaways were, in Jamaica, kept in the local workhouse until their owners came for them. In 1794, 1076 slaves were waiting to be collected. All runaways who were caught were punished severely and often killed.

SOURCE 15

1776 Jack, for being a runaway, sentenced to be immediately carried to the place of execution and there to be hanged by the neck until he is dead, and his head to be cut off in the most public place on the said estate.

1776 Adam, for running away, to be taken hence to the place from whence he came, there to have a halter put about his neck, and one of his ears nailed to a post, and that the executioner do then cause the said ear to be cut off close to his head.

1783 Priscilla, for running away, both her ears cut off close to her head immediately, to receive 39 lashes the first Monday in every month for one year and to be worked in irons during that time.

Some of the punishments in the Session Book for the parish of St Thomas in the East, Jamaica.

SOURCE 16

This treadmill, in the Jamaican Slave House of Correction, was introduced as an improvement on the older forms of slave punishments. Slaves worked it while they were waiting for their owners to collect them.

EQUIANO

Olaudah Equiano (1745–97) was taken from Africa to Barbados when he was ten years old. He ended up as the slave of Captain Pascal who sailed the Caribbean, the North Atlantic and the Mediterranean. Equiano sometimes stayed in London, rather than sailing with Pascal. The Guerin family, who he stayed with, taught him to read. In 1766 Equiano bought his freedom. He then worked for eleven years as a sailor on cargo ships.

Equiano was determined to fight slavery. In 1789 he wrote his life story, which was used by many people to argue against slavery and the slave trade. Equiano travelled around Britain speaking against slavery. He spoke in Birmingham, Sheffield, Bristol and Durham. In 1792 he married Susan Cullen, who came from Ely. They had two daughters.

Who benefited from the Slave Trade?

Britain's slave merchants made a profit of £12 million on the 2,500,000 Africans they bought and sold between 1630 and 1807. This was an enormous profit, and had a tremendous effect on the British economy and on the lives of thousands of people living and working in the ports, towns and cities of Britain. Many merchants used their money to buy themselves country estates and power and influence in parliament; others **invested** heavily in banks, insurance companies, in the cotton industry and in engineering companies. This in turn created jobs for thousands of other men and women and caused small fishing ports and market towns to grow into international trading centres. The government, too, gained from the increase in the amount of taxes and duties it levied. In 1770 the income from Jamaica alone was £1.5 million. All in all, the slave trade played a very important part in turning Britain into a powerful and rich industrial country.

SOURCE 1

This engraving is called 'Europe supported by Africa and America'. It was made by William Blake in 1796.

Which ports gained from the slave trade?

In 1700 Liverpool and Bristol were two small fishing ports. Liverpool had around 5,000 inhabitants and Bristol about 20,000. One hundred years later over 78,000 people lived and worked in Liverpool and 64,000 in Bristol. Both these small fishing ports had become flourishing and prosperous centres of international trade. Their prosperity depended on the slave trade. Bristol's wealth came from trading in slaves and slave-produced sugar; Liverpool's wealth came from trading in slaves and slave-produced cotton.

Other ports (Lancaster, Whitehaven, Portsmouth, Chester, Preston, Poulton-le-Fylde, Plymouth, Exeter, Dartmouth and Glasgow) were also involved in the slave trade. However, they were involved only in a small way. Lancaster, for example, cleared only four ships a year for slaving between 1757 and 1776; the other ports recorded fewer sailings. No British port was able to challenge the superiority of Bristol and Liverpool in the slave trade.

QUAQUE

Philip Quaque (1741–1816) was the son of Birempon Cudjo, the ruler of the Cape Coast, in Africa. He was sent to school in England in 1754 and became a Church of England priest in 1765.

Quaque married an Englishwoman, Catherine Blunt. They went to live in Africa and stayed there for fifty years. They ran a school and taught Africans about Christianity.

The first recorded voyage of a Liverpool slaver was in September 1700. A ship called the *Liverpool Merchant* sailed for the African coast. Her captain was William Webster. He delivered 220 black African slaves to Barbados where they sold for £4,239. By 1726 there were 21 ships in Liverpool's slaving fleet, and by 1757 there were 176 Liverpool-based slavers. Liverpool's slave merchants rose to positions of power and influence in the town. At least 26 of Liverpool's mayors between 1700 and 1820 were slave merchants. Thousands of people found work because of the slave trade. More and more ships were needed. These had to be built and equipped. Carpenters, rope-makers, sail-makers, dockers and sailors were all needed. Many found jobs in banking and insurance. Gradually the prosperity of the whole town and those who lived there began to depend more and more on the slave trade.

The growth and prosperity of Bristol came about in a similar way, as you can see from Sources 3 and 4.

SOURCE 2

The slave trade was the pride of Liverpool, for it flooded the town with wealth which invigorated every industry, provided the capital [money] for docks, enriched and employed the mills of Lancashire, and afforded the means for opening out new and ever new lines of trade. Beyond a doubt it was the slave trade which raised Liverpool from a struggling port to be one of the richest and most prosperous trading centres in the world.

Ramsey Muir, A History of Liverpool, 1907.

SOURCE 3

There is not a brick in the city but what is cemented with the blood of a slave. Sumptuous mansions, luxurious living and uniformed servants were the produce of the wealth made from the sufferings and groans of the slaves bought and sold by the Bristol merchants.

Written by an anonymous local historian who lived in Bristol in the 19th century.

SOURCE 4

Broad Quay, Bristol, painted in 1720.

Which industries grew because of the slave trade?

Ships leaving British ports on the first 'leg' of the Triangular Trade (look back at pages 5–7 to remind yourself what this was) took goods with them to trade for slaves. By looking at ships' **manifests**, it is fairly easy to work out which industries grew and prospered because of the slave trade. In 1787, for example, one ship's cargo consisted of guns, powder, shot, lead and iron bars, pewter basins, copper kettles and pans, iron pots, lengths of cotton and linen, silk handkerchiefs, beads, silver and gold rings, scarlet cloth, coarse blue and red woollen cloths, coarse and fine hats, worsted caps, spirits and tobacco. This was typical of all slave ships sailing at that time.

As well as carrying goods to exchange for slaves, slave ships carried goods which were needed by the Caribbean islands. In 1783, for example, Britain exported 16,576 tons of salted meat, 5,188 sides of bacon and 2,559 tons of preserved **tripe** to her Caribbean colonies. British manufacturers supplied the planters with clothes for their slaves. The ironworks of Birmingham, London, Bristol and Carron provided nails, tools and equipment for the sugar mills and boiling-houses on Caribbean sugar plantations. Travelling from the West Indies back to Britain, the slavers carried cotton, sugar, rum and tobacco. All these had to be processed once they had been off-loaded at British ports.

What was the importance of London?

By 1750 London merchants were handling about 75% of the sugar imported into Britain. They had specialized needs as far as money was concerned, and commission agents helped them whilst making a good profit themselves. The slave merchants' agents in the West Indies paid for slaves and supplies with a written note. This note promised payment of the agreed amount of money within two years. The commission agents saw that the money was paid at the right time, and took 10% for themselves. Most made a lot of money. They became part of a powerful pressure group, pushing the interests of the plantation owners in political debates and business and commerce.

SOURCE 5

The Birmingham guns of the eighteenth century were exchanged for men and it was a common saying that the price of a negro was one Birmingham gun. The African musket was an imported Birmingham export, reaching a total of 100,000–150,000 per year.

W.H.B. Court, writing in **The Rise of the Midland Industries**, *in 1938.*

SOURCE 6

If we have no Negroes, we can have no sugar, tobacco, rum etc. Consequently, the public revenue, arising from the importation of plantation-produce, would be wiped out: And will this not turn many hundreds of thousands of British manufacturers a begging?

Malachy Postlethwayt, an economist, writing in 1746.

THINK IT THROUGH

Did merchants trade in slaves in order to boost British industrial development, or was industrial prosperity an unexpected outcome of the slave trade?

A picture of the Pool of London, painted in the early nineteenth century.

In London there was a very powerful pressure group called the 'West India lobby'. This lobby was made up of three sorts of people. First there were the commission agents. Then there were the **absentee proprietors**, plantation owners who didn't live in the West Indies but lived in London. About 40 of them were MPs, and always voted in the House of Commons to support the interests of plantation owners. Finally there were the political agents of the West Indian assemblies, who were paid by the assemblies to press their interests in London. This 'West India lobby' pushed hard for what they wanted. For example, in 1763 they demanded that Canada became part of the British Empire, and not the Caribbean islands of Guadeloupe or Martinique. This was because Guadeloupe and Martinique were sugar islands, and their huge crops would have sent the London sugar prices crashing. In 1802 they succeeded in having the West India Docks, on the Isle of Dogs, constructed and opened.

Who made fortunes?

Many plantation owners made a fortune. Some of them settled in Britain on enormous country estates; others built large town houses in London. Some used their wealth to buy seats in the House of Commons and others used their money to equip libraries at Oxford University. William Beckford, a Jamaican planter, who was twice Lord Mayor of London, spent £10,000 in 1769 on a banquet where 600 dishes were served on gold plates. His two brothers and two sons were MPs. Arthur and Benjamin Heywood made their fortunes in the slave trade. They invested in the woollen industry, and founded their own bank which was later absorbed into Barclays Bank. John Gladstone invested his profits in shipping and trading, in Heywoods Bank, insurance and the Liverpool to Manchester railway. His son, William Ewart Gladstone, was four times **Prime Minister** in the nineteenth century.

EMIDY

Joseph Emidy was born in Guinea. He was sold to Portugese slavers and ended up playing the violin in a Lisbon opera house. Then, in 1795, he was captured by some British sailors who wanted him to play jigs, reels and hornpipes to dance to on their ship. They forced him to stay with them until 1799, when they put him ashore at Falmouth, Cornwall. He lived here for the rest of his life. He married Jenefer Hutchins in 1802, and they had five children. Emidy wrote music and performed in Falmouth. We do not know exactly when he was born, or when he died.

Why was the Slave Trade abolished?

You have seen how profitable the slave trade was by the middle of the eighteenth century. Yet in 1807 Parliament voted to end trading in slaves in British ships and by British merchants. Some historians say that the slave trade was abolished because of the efforts of **humanitarians** like William Wilberforce, who whipped up public opinion against the treatment of slaves so that Parliament had to act. Other historians say that the slave trade would have ended in any case, because many West Indian plantations were closing down and it was no longer necessary to buy slaves from Africa. As you work through this Unit, try to work out what you think about why the slave trade was abolished.

What did white people in Britain do to stop the slave trade?

In 1765 Granville Sharp and his brother William helped a badly beaten black youth, Jonathan Strong, until he was well enough to work again. Jonathan was a slave, and Granville Sharp was able to stop his master sending him back to the West Indies. From that time onwards, Granville became a leading **campaigner** against the slave trade. In 1772 he defended James Somerset, a slave from Virginia who had run away from his master when they were visiting England. Lord Mansfield's judgment in this case (Source 2) didn't end slavery in Britain, but it did make a lot of influential people aware of the problem.

Granville Sharp became chairman of the Society for the Abolition of the Slave Trade when it was founded by a group of **Quakers** in 1787. In 1761, the Quakers had said that anyone involved in the trade could not be a member of the **Society of Friends**. Members of the Society for the Abolition of the Slave Trade gave lectures, wrote **tracts** and newspaper articles, and did all they could to alert people up and down the country to the horrors of the slave trade.

SOURCE 1

That this House, considering the African slave trade to be contrary to the principles of justice, humanity, and sound policy, will, with all practicable expedition (speed) take effectual measure for the abolition of the said trade.

From the Bill to abolish the trade in slaves, which was introduced in Parliament on 10 June 1806.

SOURCE 2

The exercise of the power of a master over his slave must be supported by the law of particular countries; but no foreigners can in England claim a right over a man; such claim is not known to the law of England. The power claimed never was in use here, or acknowledged by the law, and therefore the man must be discharged.

Part of the judgment of Lord Mansfield, Lord Chief Justice of England, in the James Somerset case in 1772. It meant that slave owners couldn't ship their slaves out of Britain unless the slaves wanted to go.

SOURCE 3

God is no respecter of persons. Whosoever feareth Him, and worketh righteousness, is accepted of Him. And He hath made all nations of one blood.

George Fox, founder of the Quakers, in 1657.

Thomas Clarkson travelled over 35,000 miles in Britain collecting evidence of **atrocities** committed by slave traders. He interviewed ships' captains, sailors, merchants and black seamen who had once been slaves. He visited Bristol and Liverpool and other slaving ports. He set up local committees to agitate for the abolition of the slave trade, and tried to get the support of important people. One of these people was William Wilberforce, the MP for Hull, who became his friend. He led the fight in Parliament against the slave trade (see page 26).

John Newton was once the captain of a slaver (see Source 4 on page 11). He was converted to Christianity, left the sea and became Rector of St Mary Woolnoth in London. There he wrote the hymn 'Amazing Grace'. He gave evidence about the horrors of the slave trade to those campaigning against it.

(see page 26) ... (see Source 4 on page 11)

SOURCE 4

This china medallion was made in the factories of Josiah Wedgwood at Burslem in support of the anti-slavery campaign. Thousands of them were given away free in Britain, and hundreds exported to America. The inscription around the edge reads 'Am I not a man and a brother?'

SOURCE 5

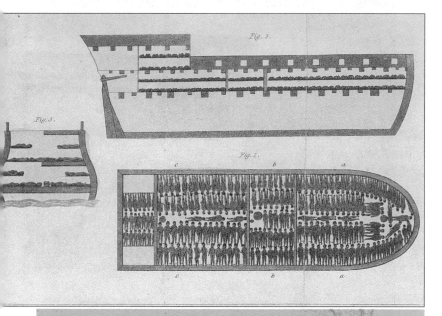

This plan of the hold of a Liverpool slave ship was drawn by Thomas Clarkson as part of the campaign against the slave trade.

THINK IT THROUGH

Propaganda is material which is spoken, written, drawn, photographed or filmed in order to persuade people to think and believe in a certain way. We usually say that propaganda is biased in one way or another.

Source 5 was drawn in order to help persuade people that the slave trade was wrong. Is it therefore biased? How could you check?

Black people in Britain

In the 18th century, about 10,000 black people lived in Britain. Some had been brought to Britain by slaver captains, hoping to make some money on the side by a quick sale; others had been brought by planters, administrators and army and navy officers who wanted to keep their own personal and household slaves because they were cheaper than servants. Slaves worked for food and clothing; servants needed wages as well. Most of the black people in Britain at this time worked in households as cooks, maids, coachmen, footmen and pages. Owning a black slave was something of a status symbol: blacks were exotic talking points in smart society.

Not all black people in Britain were slaves. Some gained their freedom when their owners died; some managed to buy theirs or had it bought for them, and some simply ran away. Black free men worked in Britain as labourers, craftsmen and seamen; some became actors and teachers. Black women worked as laundrymaids, seamstresses and children's nurses. Some became actresses and singers, and some were forced into prostitution. Others led very different lives.

In 1773 a book of 39 poems was published in London and was re-printed many times. The poems were written by a 19 year-old slave woman called Phillis Wheatley. Many important people were shocked when they discovered that such talented poems were written by a slave. Phillis lived in Boston, America, where she belonged to a tailor's wife. The tailor's wife bought her when she was about seven years old. Phillis learned to read and write in English and in Latin. In 1773 Phillis visited England with her owner's son. She met dukes and duchesses, and the Lord Mayor of London gave her a valuable edition of *Paradise Lost* by John Milton.

SOURCE 6

I cannot bear the poor wretch being ill-used; if you like him I will send him, he will be a good cheap servant and you will make a Christian of him and a good boy; if you don't like him they say Lady Rockingham wants one.

Part of a letter from Georgiana Cavendish, the Duchess of Devonshire, to her mother. The Duke of Devonshire had refused to let her keep an eleven year old black boy.

SOURCE 7

A portrait of the Duchess of Portsmouth, painted in 1682, with a black child servant.

Sixteen years later, in 1789, Olaudah Equiano wrote the story of his life. He had been a slave to a ship's captain and had travelled widely. When Equiano finally bought his freedom he returned to England to write his book. It was published in London and quickly became a best-seller. It turned many people against slavery. Equiano travelled the country speaking at meetings held to protest against slavery and the slave trade. He worked closely with Granville Sharp and other **abolitionists**.

Revolt!

In 1789 a revolution broke out in France. The revolutionary ideas of 'Liberty, Equality, Fraternity' spread to the French colonies. The plantation owners on the French West Indian island of St Domingue were terrified that their slaves would take up these new ideas, and were afraid they would revolt as the revolutionaries had done successfully in France. The planters planned an alliance with Britain. The black slaves, who lived and worked in the worst conditions in the Caribbean, knew that this would mean that slavery on the island would continue. In 1791 they burned the sugar plantations and killed plantation owners. Their leader was Toussaint L'Ouverture. Britain sent troops. In 1793 they were defeated by Toussaint, who set up an independent state.

The French were furious. In 1802 a huge French army landed in St Domingue to claim the colony back. Toussaint was captured in the fighting that followed and sent to France where he was put in prison. Meanwhile, back in St Domingue, French troops were dying in their thousands from **yellow fever**. Toussaint's generals, Christophe and Dessalines, attacked fiercely. The French surrendered, and on 1 January 1804 Dessalines declared St Domingue an independent state. The new state was called Haiti. Haiti was the first black independent state in the **New World**, and the first one to end plantation slavery.

THINK IT THROUGH

It is people who make things happen. Sometime people's actions directly influence events. Sometimes they influence them indirectly.

Which actions written about on these two pages worked behind the scenes to change people's attitudes to the slave trade, and which made people face up to what was happening in a more direct way?

SOURCE 8

This is what an artist working for a French journal thought the revolt on St Domingue would have looked like.

Economics

You read on page 25 about the slave revolt in St Domingue. Not surprisingly, whilst the slaves were busy rioting, the sugar crop rotted. From 1791 the sugar industry on St Domingue collapsed completely. This was good news as far as the British merchants were concerned. There was less sugar available for sale on the European market, and so prices rocketed. However, during the wars with France (1793–1815) Britain captured the Caribbean islands of Trinidad (1797), Tobago and St Lucia (1803). The old-established planters on the other British Caribbean colonies were worried. They were afraid that the slave trade would fill these new colonies with slaves and their sugar production would increase. The sugar market would become flooded and prices would fall. Their only solution was to back the humanitarians and support the abolition of the slave trade.

The British Caribbean colonies were, in any case, becoming less important to Britain as sugar producers. Merchants had found that they could buy sugar from Cuba and Brazil at lower prices. Many British Caribbean plantations closed down. In 1771 Barbados imported 2,728 slaves; in 1772 the island imported none at all. Merchants in Liverpool and Bristol began to move their money from the slave trade to cotton and banking. The days of the supremacy of British Caribbean sugar were at an end.

Parliament

Individual slave traders, like John Newton, (see pages 11 and 21) could get out and find another job. The Quakers could forbid any slave trader from being a member of the Society of Friends. Bristol and Liverpool merchants could move their money to a more profitable trade. But as long as there was some money to be made from slave trading, it would continue until there was a law forbidding it.

From about 1788, because of the work of men like Thomas Clarkson (see page 23) hundreds of petitions demanding the ending of the slave trade were delivered to parliament. In 1792 alone there were over 500. What was important about these petitions was that they were signed by thousands of working men and women, not just the richer people who had always had the time to take an interest in charitable movements.

SOURCE 9

Those who see in abolition the gradually awakening conscience of mankind should spend a few minutes asking themselves why it is man's conscience, which had slept peacefully for so many centuries, should awake just at the time that men began to see the unprofitableness of slavery as a method of production in the West Indian colonies.

C.L.R James, The Black Jacobins: Toussaint L'Ouverture, 1938.

SOURCE 10

Work done by slaves, though it appears to cost only their maintenance, is in the end the dearest of any. A person who can acquire no property, can have no other interest but to eat as much, and to labour as little, as possible. Whatever work he does beyond what is sufficient to purchase his own maintenance, can be squeezed out of him by violence only.

Adam Smith, a British economist, writing in 1776.

William Pitt, the Prime Minister, wanted to stop the trade in slaves, but he knew the strength of the West India lobby (see page 21). Parliament did pass the Slave Trade Regulating Act in 1788, which put a limit on the number of slaves that could be carried in British ships of certain sizes. This was not enough for William Wilberforce (see page 23). He and his supporters introduced several bills to end the slave trade, but they were all defeated. It was not until 1806 that the general climate of opinion seemed to be changing. Parliament first agreed to end the supply of slaves to islands captured from France during the French Wars. Finally, on 10 June 1806, Parliament agreed that no British subject could take part in any aspect of the slave trade. The Bill became law from 1 May 1807.

Afterwards

Britain took strict measures to make sure the slave trade stopped. Any British ship caught slaving was **impounded,** and slaver captains (or owners) paid a £100 fine for every slave found on the ship. In 1811, any British subject caught dealing in slaves could be **transported** to **penal colonies**. The British government persuaded other countries to end trading in slaves. Sweden abolished the slave trade in 1813, Holland in 1814, France in 1815, and Spain in 1820.

It was only a matter of time before slavery itself was abolished. Public opinion and riots in the Caribbean colonies pushed Parliament in 1833 into agreeing to a bill which abolished slavery in the British Empire from 1 August 1834. The government made £20 million available to compensate the slave owners. This was about £37 per slave. The slaves themselves first had to work an apprenticeship system, whereby they were only partly free. This ended in 1838. From that time onwards there was no slavery anywhere in the British Empire.

A painting showing slaves in Barbados celebrating their independence in 1838.

WILBERFORCE

William Wilberforce (1759–1833) was an MP and also an evangelical Christian. In 1788, with the help of Thomas Clarkson and the Quakers, he began a campaign against the slave trade and slavery. In 1791 Wilberforce tried to get Parliament to pass a law abolishing the slave trade. He kept trying. In 1804 the House of Commons accepted it, but not the House of Lords. It finally became a law in 1807. Wilberforce then tried to get slavery abolished altogether. Slavery in the British Empire ended in 1833.

A Mystery

This is a real mystery, and one which cropped up whilst this book was being written. The publisher and the author think they might have almost solved it, but there are quite a few questions that are still not answered. Maybe you can do some real historical research and get even nearer to the truth of what actually happened. Remember – this mystery has not yet been solved. Your solution, provided it fits in with the evidence, is as likely to be correct as that which anyone else can provide.

The mystery began with the picture the publishers chose for the front cover. Look at it now. It seemed ideal for the front cover of a book called 'Britain and the Slave Trade'. The publishers had used the painting before, in another book, and part of the caption to the picture said 'Slaves below deck, painted by a British naval officer in 1818'.

Problem 1: *The slave trade ended in 1807*

The publishers checked with the National Maritime Museum in Greenwich. They suggested that the date 1818 was wrong. They sent a copy of two of their record cards which you can see here as Source 1.

Problem 2: *Is the date of 1820 any more likely to be correct?*

The National Maritime Museum suggested 1845 as a more likely date for the painting because that was the date on which the slave ship *Albaroz* was captured.

Problem 3: *Can we be sure the slave ship in the painting is the **Albaroz**?*

Now read Source 2.

Problem 4: *Can we be sure Lt. Meynell served on HMS **Albatross?***

Now read Source 3. Does this help answer problem 4? Finally, read the newspaper cutting (Source 4) very carefully. It is from a collection of cuttings Lt. Meynell sent to his father.

Problem 5: *Does Source 4 refer to the capture of the **Albaroz?***

SOURCE 1

SLAVE DECK AND SLAVE INTERIOR

Negative A1817: Slaves on deck of the 'Albaroz', prize to HMS 'Albatross'

Negative A1818: Interior slave deck of the 'Albaroz

Artist: Lt. Francis Meynell (watercolour)

SLAVE SHIP – Dated about 1820

Drawings of deck and slaves below deck in journal of Lt. Meynell.

Below deck – Negative (CT) A1818

Above deck – Negative A1817

Two record cards from the National Maritime Museum at Greenwich.

SOURCE 2

Between 1844 and 1845 he [Lieutenant Francis Meynell] was a mate in the **Penelope** during the anti-slavery operations off the coast of Africa.

*From **Guide to the Manuscripts in the National Maritime Museum**.*

SOURCE 3

I have located a manuscript in our collection which states that Meynell served as mate on board HMS **Albatross** from 29 November 1844 to 27 May 1845 during which period the slave brig **Albaroz** was captured and Meynell was entitled to a share of the prize money. Enclosed is a copy of a newspaper cutting from the collection of cuttings and letters Meynell sent to his father while on active service. It may refer to the capture of **Albaroz**.

Part of a letter from the National Maritime Museum at Greenwich to Heinemann, the publishers.

ACTIVITIES

Can you now answer these questions?

1 **What does the painting on the front cover of this book show?**

2 **Who painted it?**

3 **When was the picture painted?**

   How certain are you of the accuracy of these answers?

4 **What have you learned about the survival of the slave trade from trying to 'solve' the mystery of the painting?**

SOURCE 4

Extraordinary capture of a slave vessel

We have just received a letter from an officer of the **Albatross,** Captain R. Yorke, describing the capture of a slave brig, on the 1st March, off the Congo River, on the coast of West Africa.

'On the 28th February we saw what we thought was a vessel lying close to land, near the River Congo. The weather was rather hazy. It appeared to us that the vessel was on fire, so we lowered down a rowing boat and sent her to find out which nation the vessel belonged to. Meanwhile we sailed in close to the land and anchored about seven miles to the south of the river. At daylight we spotted a brig to the northward and sailed to investigate. As we neared we saw several boats sailing to and fro, and two objects in shore, which appeared to be wrecks which had burned down to the water's edge. Then we saw our rowing boat board the brig, but she shortly afterwards left her again and pulled in towards the land in the direction of what we thought to be the wrecks. One or two guns were fired at our boat from the shore, which the boat's crew returned. Shortly afterwards we saw our red ensign flying at the vessel's mast-head which gave us all hope that it was a prize. We now realised that what we took to be the wrecks were two rafts, made of water casks, each carrying 200 slaves, which the brig was in the act of taking on board.

The brig was 250 tons and had already taken on 300 negroes when we arrived on the scene. If we had been a day later she would have taken on a full cargo of 743 and been on her way to Brazil. A supply of water and provisions, as well as slave irons, was also on its way, but our arrival caused the canoe conveying it to pull back. Our boats took the slaves off the rafts and carried them on board the slave brig. The Portuguese captain and crew had already deserted the vessel in great haste.

We carried our prize to Luanda.'

Part of a newspaper cutting sent by Lt. Meynell to his father.

Glossary

abolitionist a person who wanted to abolish the slave trade.

absentee proprietor a person who owned land in the Caribbean but did not live there.

acre an area of land: 2.471 acres = 1 hectare.

agent someone who works on behalf of another and is usually paid for doing so.

Assembly a meeting of all the important people in a colony to decide how the colony would be run. Any decisions made had to be agreed to by Parliament in London.

atrocity a wicked or cruel act.

auction a sale of slaves where buyers said out loud how much they were prepared to pay, and pushed the price up by trying to outbid (offer more money than) another buyer.

boatswain a ship's officer in charge of the crew.

bow the front of a ship.

British West Indies Caribbean islands which were colonies of Britain.

campaigner a person who works hard on behalf of something they believe in.

chattels belongings.

colony an island or land which was not independent but which was ruled by another country. Usually that country had conquered the colony.

creoles slaves who were born in the West Indies.

dropsy a disease where a watery fluid collects in the body.

dysentery very bad diarrhoea, as a result of a person's bowel becoming inflamed.

English creole a language, similar to English, spoken by creoles.

gangs groups of slave workers.

god-parent an adult slave who took responsibility for a younger slave who did not have any parents.

heat stroke an illness caused by staying too long in the sun.

hold the space below a ship's deck where cargo is put.

horse-bean a bean rather like a red kidney bean which was eaten in Africa.

humanitarian a person who tries to work for the good of other people.

impounded taken away and kept by the authorities, usually until the owner pays a fine.

inoculate treat with a vaccine in order to prevent an illness.

invest put money into a business or company in the hope of eventually making a profit.

manifest a list of goods carried as cargo or people carried as passengers.

Maroons people who were descended from slaves who ran away when the British first invaded Jamaica in 1655.

middlemen people who bought goods or slaves from one merchant and sold them on to another.

Middle Passage part of the Triangular Trade where black Africans were carried as cargo from Africa to the Caribbean.

molasses thick, black or dark brown syrup drained from raw sugar.

mulatto slave with one black parent and one white parent.

mutiny open revolt against authority.

Navigation Laws a series of laws passed by Parliament which controlled what British ships could do.

New World America and the Caribbean islands.

overseer a person, usually a slave, who was put in charge of gangs of slaves to get a jobdone.

penal colonies colonies (e.g. Australia) to which criminals were sent as part of their sentence.

plantation the entire estate (land and buildings) belonging to a planter and his family.

planters men who owned plantations in the West Indies.

portholes round windows in the sides of a ship.

Prime Minister the minister who leads the government.

private treaty an legally binding agreement made between private individuals.

Quaker a member of the Society of Friends, people who worshipped God without organized Church services.

refuse slaves slaves who were left behind, unsold, after an auction.

second mate the second most important officer on a merchant ship.

slavers ships that carried slaves, or people involved in the slave trade.

slaves people who were regarded as belonging to their owners.

smallpox a serious disease with fevers and pus-filled spots which could scar for life.

Society of Friends Quakers.

stern the back of a ship.

tract a pamphlet.

transported taken by ship to a penal colony like Australia.

Triangular Trade trade involving three stages: (i) goods from Britain to Africa (ii) slaves from Africa to the Caribbean (iii) goods from the Caribbean to Britain.

tripe stomach of a cow or ox used as food for humans.

underground railroad various routes whereby runaway slaves were helped to get to the northern states of the USA where slavery was illegal and they would be free.

West Indies Caribbean islands.

yams sweet potatoes.

yaws a tropical skin disease.

yellow fever a tropical disease with jaundice, which turns a person's skin yellow.

NB Some of the words in this glossary (for example, **manifest**) have more than one meaning. The meaning given here is the meaning which relates to the Slave Trade and the one which is used in this book.

Index